ONE POT

Cooking

D1396774

pil

Publications International, Ltd.

Let's get social!

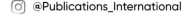 @Publications_International

 @PublicationsInternational

www.pilbooks.com

Contents

Dutch Oven

SPICY CHICKEN RIGATONI

2 tablespoons olive oil

2 cloves garlic, minced

½ teaspoon red pepper flakes

½ teaspoon black pepper

8 ounces boneless skinless chicken breasts, cut into thin strips

1 cup marinara sauce

¾ cup prepared Alfredo sauce

1 package (16 ounces) uncooked rigatoni or penne pasta, cooked until al dente

¾ cup frozen peas, thawed

Grated Parmesan cheese (optional)

1. Heat oil in Dutch oven over medium-high heat. Add garlic, red pepper flakes and black pepper; cook and stir 1 minute. Add chicken; cook and stir 4 minutes or until cooked through.

2. Add marinara sauce and Alfredo sauce; stir until blended. Reduce heat to medium-low; cook 10 minutes, stirring occasionally.

3. Add pasta and peas; stir gently to coat. Cook 2 minutes or until heated through. Sprinkle with cheese, if desired.

Makes 4 servings

PASTA FAGIOLI

2 tablespoons olive oil, divided

1 pound ground beef

1 cup chopped onion

1 cup diced carrots

1 cup diced celery

3 cloves garlic, minced

4 cups beef broth

1 can (28 ounces) diced tomatoes

1 can (15 ounces) tomato sauce

1 tablespoon cider vinegar

2 teaspoons sugar

1½ teaspoons dried basil

1¼ teaspoons salt

1 teaspoon dried oregano

¾ teaspoon dried thyme

2 cups uncooked ditalini pasta

1 can (about 15 ounces) dark red kidney beans, rinsed and drained

1 can (about 15 ounces) cannellini beans, rinsed and drained

Grated Romano cheese (optional)

1. Heat 1 tablespoon oil in Dutch oven over medium-high heat. Add beef; cook 5 minutes or until browned, stirring to break up meat. Remove to medium bowl. Drain fat.

2. Add remaining 1 tablespoon oil to Dutch oven; heat over medium-high heat. Add onion, carrots and celery; cook and stir 5 minutes or until vegetables are tender. Add garlic; cook and stir 1 minute. Add cooked beef, broth, tomatoes, tomato sauce, vinegar, sugar, basil, salt, oregano and thyme; bring to a boil. Reduce heat to medium-low; cover and simmer 30 minutes.

3. Add pasta, kidney beans and cannellini beans; cook over medium heat 10 minutes or until pasta is tender, stirring frequently. Top with cheese, if desired.

Makes 8 servings

TEX-MEX BLACK BEAN AND CORN STEW

1 tablespoon canola or vegetable oil

1 small onion, chopped

4 cloves garlic, minced

1 teaspoon chili powder

1 teaspoon ground cumin

½ teaspoon salt

1 can (about 14 ounces) fire-roasted diced tomatoes

¾ cup salsa

2 medium zucchini or yellow squash (or 1 of each), cut into ½-inch chunks

1 can (about 15 ounces) black beans, rinsed and drained

1 cup frozen corn

½ cup (2 ounces) shredded Cheddar or pepper jack cheese

¼ cup chopped fresh cilantro or green onion

1. Heat oil in Dutch oven over medium heat. Add onion; cook and stir 5 minutes. Add garlic, chili powder, cumin and salt; cook and stir 1 minute.

2. Stir in tomatoes, salsa, zucchini, black beans and corn; bring to a boil over high heat. Reduce heat to low; cover and cook 20 minutes or until vegetables are tender. Top with cheese and cilantro.

Makes 4 servings

HAM JAMBALAYA

2 tablespoons butter

1 onion, chopped

½ cup thinly sliced celery

½ red bell pepper, diced

2 cloves garlic, minced

1 jar (about 16 ounces) medium salsa

2 cups cubed cooked ham

1 cup uncooked long grain rice

1 cup water

⅔ cup vegetable broth

3 teaspoons prepared horseradish

2 teaspoons honey

¼ to ½ teaspoon hot pepper sauce

1½ pounds medium or large raw shrimp, peeled and deveined

1 tablespoon chopped fresh mint

1. Preheat oven to 350°F.

2. Melt butter in Dutch oven over medium heat. Add onion, celery, bell pepper and garlic; cook and stir 3 minutes or until vegetables are tender. Stir in salsa, ham, rice, water, broth, horseradish, honey and hot pepper sauce; mix well.

3. Cover and bake 40 minutes or until rice is almost tender.

4. Stir in shrimp and mint; bake 10 to 15 minutes or until shrimp are pink and opaque.

Makes 6 to 8 servings

HEARTY TUSCAN SOUP

1 teaspoon olive oil

1 pound bulk mild or hot Italian sausage*

1 medium onion, chopped

3 cloves garlic, minced

¼ cup all-purpose flour

5 cups chicken broth

1 teaspoon salt

½ teaspoon Italian seasoning

2 large unpeeled russet potatoes (about 1 pound), halved lengthwise and thinly sliced

2 cups packed torn stemmed kale

1 cup half-and-half or whipping cream

Or use sausage links and remove from casings.

1. Heat oil in Dutch oven over medium-high heat. Add sausage; cook until sausage begins to brown, stirring to break up meat. Add onion and garlic; cook about 5 minutes or until onion is softened and sausage is browned, stirring occasionally.

2. Stir in flour until blended. Add broth, salt and Italian seasoning; bring to a boil. Stir in potatoes and kale. Reduce heat to medium-low; cook 15 to 20 minutes or until potatoes are fork-tender.

3. Reduce heat to low; stir in half and half. Cook about 5 minutes or until heated through.

Makes 6 to 8 servings

CHICKEN CASSOULET

4	slices bacon
¼	cup all-purpose flour
	Salt and black pepper
1¾	pounds bone-in chicken pieces
2	chicken sausages (2¼ ounces each), cooked and cut into ¼-inch pieces
1½	cups diced red and green bell peppers
1	medium onion, chopped
2	cloves garlic, minced
1	teaspoon dried thyme
1	to 2 teaspoons olive oil
½	cup dry white wine
2	cans (about 15 ounces each) cannellini or Great Northern beans, rinsed and drained

1. Preheat oven to 350°F.

2. Cook bacon in Dutch oven over medium-high heat until crisp; drain on paper towel-lined plate. Cut into 1-inch pieces.

3. Place flour in shallow bowl; season with salt and black pepper. Coat chicken pieces with flour mixture; shake off excess. Brown chicken in batches in Dutch oven over medium-high heat; remove to plate. Lightly brown sausages in Dutch oven; remove to plate.

4. Add bell peppers, onion, garlic and thyme to Dutch oven; cook and stir over medium heat 5 minutes or until softened, adding oil as needed to prevent sticking. Stir in wine, scraping up browned bits from bottom of pan. Stir in beans; mix well. Top with chicken, sausages and bacon.

5. Cover and bake 40 minutes. Uncover; bake 15 minutes or until chicken is cooked through (165°F).

Makes 6 servings

VEGETARIAN CHILI

2 tablespoons olive oil

1 onion, finely chopped

2 medium carrots, chopped

1 red bell pepper, chopped

3 tablespoons chili powder

2 tablespoons ground cumin

2 tablespoons tomato paste

2 tablespoons packed dark brown sugar

3 cloves garlic, minced

1 tablespoon dried oregano

1 teaspoon salt

1 can (28 ounces) diced tomatoes

1 can (15 ounces) tomato sauce

1 can (about 15 ounces) small white beans, rinsed and drained

1 can (about 15 ounces) light kidney beans, rinsed and drained

1 can (about 15 ounces) dark kidney beans, rinsed and drained

1 can (about 15 ounces) pinto beans, rinsed and drained

1 cup vegetable broth

1 can (4 ounces) diced mild green chiles

1 ounce unsweetened baking chocolate, chopped

1 tablespoon cider vinegar

1. Heat oil in Dutch oven over medium-high heat. Add onion, carrots and bell pepper; cook 10 minutes or until vegetables are tender, stirring frequently. Add chili powder, cumin, tomato paste, brown sugar, garlic, oregano and salt; cook and stir 1 minute.

2. Stir in tomatoes, tomato sauce, beans, broth, chiles and chocolate; bring to a boil. Reduce heat to medium; cook 20 minutes, stirring occasionally. Stir in vinegar.

Makes 8 to 10 servings

POZOLE

3 (6-inch) corn tortillas

1 tablespoon vegetable oil

1 large onion, chopped

1 tablespoon minced garlic

1 tablespoon dried oregano

1½ teaspoons ground cumin

2 cans (about 14 ounces each) chicken broth

1½ cups water

1 pound boneless skinless chicken breasts

2 cans (about 15 ounces each) yellow hominy, drained

1 red or green bell pepper, chopped

1 can (4 ounces) diced mild green chiles

1 can (2¼ ounces) sliced black olives, drained

½ cup lightly packed fresh cilantro, coarsely chopped

1. Preheat oven to 450°F.

2. Cut tortillas into ¼-inch-wide strips. Place strips in single layer on baking sheet. Bake 3 to 4 minutes or until crisp. (Do not let strips brown.) Remove to plate to cool.

3. Heat oil in Dutch oven over medium heat. Add onion, garlic, oregano and cumin; cook and stir about 6 minutes or until onion is golden brown, stirring occasionally. Add broth and water; bring to a boil. Stir in chicken. Reduce heat to low; cover and cook 8 minutes or until chicken is no longer pink in center. Remove chicken to plate; set aside until cool enough to handle. Cut into ½-inch pieces.

4. Meanwhile, add hominy, bell pepper, chiles and olives to broth in Dutch oven; bring to a boil over medium-high heat. Reduce heat to medium-low; cover and cook 4 minutes or until bell pepper is crisp-tender. Return chicken to Dutch oven with cilantro; cook just until heated through. Top with toasted tortilla strips.

Makes 6 servings

CHICKEN AND GNOCCHI SOUP

¼ cup (½ stick) butter

1 tablespoon extra virgin olive oil

1 cup finely diced onion

2 stalks celery, finely chopped

2 cloves garlic, minced

¼ cup all-purpose flour

4 cups half-and-half

1 can (about 14 ounces) chicken broth

1 teaspoon salt

½ teaspoon dried thyme

½ teaspoon dried parsley flakes

¼ teaspoon ground nutmeg

1 package (about 16 ounces) gnocchi

1 cup diced cooked chicken

1 cup shredded carrots

1 cup coarsely chopped fresh spinach

1. Melt butter in Dutch oven over medium heat; add oil. Add onion, celery and garlic; cook about 8 minutes or until vegetables are softened and onion is translucent, stirring occasionally.

2. Whisk in flour; cook and stir about 1 minute. Whisk in half-and-half; cook about 15 minutes or until thickened, stirring occasionally.

3. Whisk in broth, salt, thyme, parsley flakes and nutmeg; cook 10 minutes or until soup is slightly thickened, stirring occasionally. Add gnocchi, chicken, carrots and spinach; cook about 5 minutes or until gnocchi are heated through.

Makes 6 to 8 servings

FETTUCCINE WITH VEGETABLE MARINARA SAUCE

2 tablespoons extra virgin olive oil

1 medium onion, finely chopped

1 small carrot, finely chopped

1 small stalk celery, finely chopped

2 cloves garlic, finely chopped

1 can (28 ounces) peeled plum tomatoes, undrained

½ cup water

⅓ cup packed chopped fresh basil leaves

Salt and black pepper

1 package (16 ounces) uncooked fettuccine, cooked and drained

Grated Parmesan cheese

1. Heat oil in Dutch oven over medium heat. Add onion, carrot, celery and garlic; cover and cook about 5 minutes or until onion is tender, stirring occasionally.

2. Drain tomatoes, reserving juice. Coarsely crush tomatoes with fingers or wooden spoon. Add tomatoes, reserved juice and water to Dutch oven; bring to a boil over high heat. Reduce heat to medium-low; cook, uncovered, about 45 minutes or until sauce is slightly thickened and reduced, stirring frequently. Stir in basil during last 5 minutes of cooking. Season with salt and pepper.

3. Serve sauce over pasta; top with Parmesan cheese.

Makes 4 to 6 servings

CORNED BEEF AND CABBAGE

3½ to 4 pounds packaged corned beef brisket

3 carrots, peeled and cut into 1½-inch pieces

1 bunch fresh parsley

2 large sprigs fresh thyme

1 head green cabbage (about 2 pounds), cut into 8 wedges

1½ pounds unpeeled small red potatoes, quartered

1 cup sour cream

2 tablespoons prepared horseradish

½ teaspoon coarse salt

Chopped fresh parsley (optional)

1. Combine corned beef and carrots in Dutch oven. Tie parsley and thyme together with kitchen string; add to Dutch oven. Add water to cover beef by 1 inch; bring to a boil over high heat. Reduce heat to medium-low; cover and cook about 2½ hours or until beef is almost tender.

2. Add cabbage and potatoes to Dutch oven; cover and cook about 30 minutes or until beef, cabbage and potatoes are tender.

3. Meanwhile, combine sour cream, horseradish and ½ teaspoon salt in medium bowl; mix well. Refrigerate until ready to serve.

4. Remove herbs from Dutch oven and discard. Remove beef to cutting board; let stand 10 minutes. Slice beef across the grain. Arrange on serving platter with vegetables; season vegetables with additional salt to taste. Sprinkle with chopped parsley, if desired; serve with horseradish sauce.

Makes 8 servings

FORTY-CLOVE CHICKEN FILICE

¼ cup olive oil

1 cut-up whole chicken (about 3 pounds)

40 cloves garlic (about 2 heads), peeled

4 stalks celery, thickly sliced

½ cup dry white wine

¼ cup dry vermouth

Grated peel and juice of 1 lemon

2 tablespoons finely chopped fresh parsley

2 teaspoons dried basil

1 teaspoon dried oregano, crushed

Pinch red pepper flakes

Salt and black pepper

1. Preheat oven to 375°F.

2. Heat oil in Dutch oven. Add chicken; cook until browned on all sides.

3. Combine garlic, celery, wine, vermouth, lemon juice, parsley, basil, oregano and red pepper flakes in medium bowl; pour over chicken. Sprinkle with lemon peel; season with salt and black pepper.

4. Cover and bake 40 minutes. Remove cover; bake 15 minutes or until chicken is cooked through (165°F).

Makes 4 to 6 servings

Baking Dish

PIZZA CHICKEN BAKE

3½ cups uncooked bowtie pasta, cooked until al dente

1 tablespoon vegetable oil

1 cup sliced mushrooms

1 jar (26 ounces) herb-flavored pasta sauce

1 teaspoon pizza seasoning blend

12 ounces boneless skinless chicken breasts, cut into 2-inch pieces

1 cup (4 ounces) shredded mozzarella cheese

1. Preheat oven to 350°F. Spray 2-quart round baking dish with nonstick cooking spray. Place pasta in prepared dish.

2. Heat oil in large skillet over medium-high heat. Add mushrooms; cook and stir 5 minutes. Add pasta sauce and pizza seasoning; mix well.

3. Pour half of pasta sauce mixture into baking dish; stir gently to coat. Top with chicken and remaining pasta sauce mixture.

4. Cover and bake 50 minutes or until chicken is cooked through. Sprinkle with cheese; cover and let stand 5 minutes before serving.

Makes 4 servings

TIP Serve with grated Parmesan cheese and red pepper flakes so everyone can add their own individual pizza seasonings.

ZUCCHINI WITH FETA CASSEROLE

4 medium zucchini

1 tablespoon butter

2 eggs, beaten

½ cup grated Parmesan cheese

⅓ cup crumbled feta cheese

2 tablespoons chopped fresh parsley

1 tablespoon all-purpose flour

2 teaspoons chopped fresh marjoram or oregano

Dash hot pepper sauce

Salt and black pepper

1. Preheat oven to 375°F. Spray 2-quart baking dish with nonstick cooking spray.

2. Grate zucchini; drain in colander. Melt butter in large skillet over medium heat. Add zucchini; cook and stir until slightly browned.

3. Remove from heat; stir in eggs, Parmesan, feta, parsley, flour, marjoram, hot pepper sauce, salt and black pepper until well blended. Pour into prepared baking dish.

4. Bake 35 minutes or until hot and bubbly.

Makes 4 servings

RAMEN REUBEN NOODLE BAKE

3 packages (3 ounces each) beef-flavored ramen noodles, cooked 2 minutes with seasoning packets and drained

2 cans (about 14 ounces each) shredded sauerkraut, undrained

1 pound thinly sliced deli corned beef, chopped

¼ cup (½ stick) butter, melted

1½ teaspoons caraway seeds, divided

½ cup Thousand Island dressing

8 slices (6 ounces) Swiss cheese

1. Preheat oven to 350°F. Spray 13×9-inch baking dish with nonstick cooking spray.

2. Combine noodles, sauerkraut with liquid, corned beef, butter and 1 teaspoon caraway seeds in large bowl; stir gently to coat. Transfer to prepared baking dish.

3. Cover and bake 20 minutes or until heated through. Drizzle with dressing; top with cheese and remaining ½ teaspoon caraway seeds. Bake, uncovered, 13 to 15 minutes or until cheese is melted and casserole is bubbly.

Makes 8 servings

BEEF, BEAN AND PASTA CASSEROLE

1 **pound ground beef**

1 **medium onion, diced**

2 **cloves garlic, minced**

1 **can (about 15 ounces) cannellini beans, rinsed and drained**

1 **can (about 14 ounces) diced tomatoes, drained**

1 **can (8 ounces) tomato sauce**

2 **teaspoons Italian seasoning**

¾ **teaspoon salt**

¼ **teaspoon black pepper**

3 **cups uncooked whole wheat rigatoni pasta, cooked until al dente**

1 **cup finely shredded Parmesan cheese**

1 **cup (4 ounces) shredded mozzarella cheese**

1. Preheat oven to 350°F. Spray 11×7-inch baking dish with nonstick cooking spray.

2. Cook beef, onion and garlic in large skillet over medium-high heat 6 to 8 minutes or until beef is browned, stirring to break up meat. Drain fat. Add beans, tomatoes, tomato sauce, Italian seasoning, salt and pepper; cook 3 minutes.

3. Remove from heat; stir in pasta and Parmesan. Transfer to prepared baking dish; sprinkle with mozzarella.

4. Bake 20 minutes or until cheese is melted and casserole is bubbly.

Makes 6 servings

VARIATIONS Any short-shape pasta can be used in this recipe. Red kidney beans can be used in place of the cannellini beans.

SPLIT-BISCUIT CHICKEN PIE

⅓ cup butter

⅓ cup all-purpose flour

2½ cups whole milk

1 tablespoon chicken bouillon granules

½ teaspoon dried thyme

½ teaspoon black pepper

4 cups diced cooked chicken

2 jars (4 ounces each) diced pimientos

1 cup frozen green peas, thawed

1 package (6 ounces) refrigerated biscuit dough, prepared according to package directions

1. Preheat oven to 350°F. Spray 2-quart or 12×8-inch baking dish with nonstick cooking spray.

2. Melt butter in large skillet over medium heat. Add flour; whisk until smooth. Add milk, bouillon, thyme and pepper; stir until well blended. Cook and stir until thickened. Remove from heat; stir in chicken, pimientos and peas. Transfer to prepared baking dish.

3. Bake 30 minutes. Split biscuits in half; arrange cut sides down over chicken mixture. Bake 3 minutes or until biscuits are heated through.

Makes 4 to 5 servings

CREAMY SHRIMP AND VEGETABLE CASSEROLE

1 **pound fresh or thawed frozen medium raw shrimp, peeled and deveined**

1 **can (10¾ ounces) condensed cream of celery soup, undiluted**

½ **cup sliced fresh or thawed frozen asparagus (1-inch pieces)**

½ **cup sliced mushrooms**

¼ **cup diced red bell pepper**

¼ **cup sliced green onions**

1 **clove garlic, minced**

¾ **teaspoon dried thyme**

¼ **teaspoon black pepper**

Hot cooked rice or orzo (optional)

1. Preheat oven to 375°F. Spray 2-quart baking dish with nonstick cooking spray.

2. Combine shrimp, soup, asparagus, mushrooms, bell pepper, green onions, garlic, thyme and black pepper in large bowl; mix well. Transfer to prepared baking dish.

3. Cover and bake 30 minutes. Serve over rice, if desired.

Makes 4 servings

BOWTIE ZUCCHINI

¼ cup olive oil

1 cup chopped onion

2 cloves garlic, minced

5 small zucchini, cut into thin strips

⅔ cup whipping cream

1 package (16 ounces) uncooked bowtie pasta, cooked until al dente

¼ cup grated Parmesan cheese

Salt and black pepper

1. Preheat oven to 350°F. Spray 2-quart baking dish with nonstick cooking spray.

2. Heat oil in large skillet over medium-high heat. Add onion and garlic; cook and stir 3 minutes or until onion is translucent. Add zucchini; cook and stir until tender.

3. Add cream; cook and stir until thickened. Add pasta and cheese to skillet; season with salt and pepper. Transfer to prepared baking dish.

4. Cover and bake 15 minutes or until heated through.

Makes 8 servings

SAUSAGE AND POLENTA CASEROLE

1 tablespoon olive oil
1 cup chopped mushrooms
1 red bell pepper, diced
1 onion, diced
1 pound bulk Italian sausage
1 jar (28 to 30 ounces) pasta sauce
1 roll (16 to 18 ounces) polenta
¼ cup shredded Parmesan cheese

1. Preheat oven to 350°F. Spray 8-inch square baking dish with nonstick cooking spray.

2. Heat oil in large skillet over medium heat. Add mushrooms, bell pepper and onion; cook and stir 5 minutes or until vegetables are tender. Add sausage; cook and stir until sausage is browned, breaking meat into small pieces with spoon. Drain fat. Stir in pasta sauce; cook 5 minutes, stirring occasionally.

3. Cut polenta crosswise into 9 slices; arrange in prepared baking dish. Top with sausage mixture.

4. Bake 15 minutes or until heated through. Sprinkle with cheese.

Makes 4 servings

HAM AND CHEESE BREAD PUDDING

1 small loaf
   (8 ounces)
   sourdough,
   country French
   or Italian bread,
   sliced
3 tablespoons
   butter, softened
8 ounces ham or
   smoked ham,
   cubed
1 cup (4 ounces)
   shredded
   Cheddar cheese
3 eggs
2 cups milk
1 teaspoon ground
   mustard
½ teaspoon salt
⅛ teaspoon white
   pepper

1. Spray 11×7-inch baking dish with nonstick cooking spray. Spread one side of each bread slice with butter. Cut into 1-inch cubes; place on bottom of prepared baking dish. Top with ham; sprinkle with cheese.

2. Beat eggs in medium bowl. Whisk in milk, mustard, salt and pepper until blended. Pour egg mixture evenly over bread mixture; cover and refrigerate at least 6 hours or overnight.

3. Preheat oven to 350°F. Bake bread pudding, uncovered, 45 to 50 minutes or until puffed and golden brown and knife inserted into center comes out clean. Serve immediately.

Makes 8 servings

Skillet

CHICKEN SAUSAGE AND TWO-GRAIN SKILLET

1   tablespoon olive oil

1   package (12 ounces) fully cooked chicken apple sausage links, cut into ½-inch slices

1   can (about 14 ounces) chicken broth

1   cup instant brown rice

½   cup uncooked quinoa

1   red bell pepper, cut into thin strips

1   stalk celery, sliced diagonally

1½   teaspoons curry powder *or* 1 teaspoon ground turmeric

½   cup thawed frozen peas

¼   cup finely chopped green onions (optional)

1. Heat oil in large skillet over medium-high heat. Add sausage; cook 3 minutes or until edges are browned, stirring occasionally.

2. Stir in broth, rice, quinoa, bell pepper, celery and curry powder; bring to a boil. Reduce heat to low; cover and cook 12 minutes or until liquid is absorbed.

3. Remove from heat; stir in peas. Let stand 5 minutes before serving. Sprinkle with green onions, if desired.

Makes 4 servings

JAMBALAYA PASTA

1 pound boneless skinless chicken breasts, cut into 1-inch pieces

2 tablespoons plus 1 teaspoon Cajun spice blend, divided

1 tablespoon vegetable oil

8 ounces bell peppers (red, yellow, green or a combination), cut into ¼-inch strips

½ medium red onion, cut into ¼-inch strips

6 ounces medium raw shrimp, peeled and deveined

2 cloves garlic, minced

1 teaspoon salt

¼ teaspoon black pepper

1½ pounds plum tomatoes (about 6), cut into ½-inch pieces

1 cup chicken broth

1 package (16 ounces) fresh or dried linguini, cooked until al dente

Chopped fresh parsley

1. Combine chicken and 2 tablespoons Cajun seasoning in medium bowl; toss to coat. Heat oil in large skillet over medium-high heat. Add chicken; cook and stir 3 minutes.

2. Add bell peppers and onion; cook and stir 3 minutes. Add shrimp, garlic, remaining 1 teaspoon Cajun seasoning, salt and black pepper; cook and stir 1 minute.

3. Stir in tomatoes and broth; bring to a boil. Reduce heat to medium-low; cook 3 minutes or until shrimp are pink and opaque. Serve over hot pasta; sprinkle with parsley.

Makes 4 servings

MEXICAN TURKEY SKILLET

1 tablespoon vegetable oil

12 ounces ground turkey

1 can (about 14 ounces) stewed tomatoes

½ (16-ounce) package frozen bell pepper stir-fry blend, thawed

¾ teaspoon ground cumin

½ teaspoon salt

½ cup (2 ounces) finely shredded sharp Cheddar cheese

2 ounces tortilla chips, broken

1. Heat oil in large skillet over medium heat. Add turkey; cook until no longer pink, stirring to break up meat.

2. Stir in tomatoes, bell peppers, cumin and salt; bring to a boil. Reduce heat to low; cover and cook 20 minutes or until vegetables are tender.

3. Sprinkle with cheese and chips.

Makes 4 servings

CHICKEN FRIED RICE

2 tablespoons vegetable oil, divided

12 ounces boneless skinless chicken breasts, cut into ½-inch pieces

Salt and black pepper

2 tablespoons butter

2 cloves garlic, minced

½ sweet onion, diced

1 medium carrot, diced

2 green onions, thinly sliced

3 eggs

4 cups cooked white rice*

3 tablespoons soy sauce

2 tablespoons sesame seeds

For rice, cook 1½ cups white rice according to package directions without oil or butter. Spread hot rice on large rimmed baking sheet; cool to room temperature. Refrigerate several hours or overnight. Measure 4 cups.

1. Heat 1 tablespoon oil in large skillet over medium-high heat. Add chicken; season with salt and pepper. Cook and stir 5 to 6 minutes or until cooked through. Add butter and garlic; cook and stir 1 minute or until butter is melted. Remove to small bowl.

2. Add sweet onion, carrot and green onions to skillet; cook and stir over high heat 3 minutes or until vegetables are softened. Add to bowl with chicken.

3. Heat remaining 1 tablespoon oil in same skillet. Crack eggs into skillet; cook and stir 45 seconds or until eggs are scrambled but still moist.

4. Add chicken and vegetable mixture, rice, soy sauce and sesame seeds to skillet; cook and stir 2 minutes or until well blended and heated through. Season with additional salt and pepper.

Makes 4 servings

TUSCAN LAMB SKILLET

8 lamb rib chops
(1½ pounds
total), 1 inch
thick

2 teaspoons olive
oil

3 teaspoons minced
garlic

1 can (19 ounces)
cannellini beans,
rinsed and
drained

1 can (about
14 ounces)
Italian-style
tomatoes,
broken up,
undrained

1 tablespoon
balsamic vinegar

2 teaspoons minced
fresh rosemary

Additional fresh
rosemary
(optional)

1. Trim fat from lamb chops. Heat oil in large skillet over medium heat. Add lamb; cook about 4 minutes per side or until 160°F for medium doneness. Remove lamb to plate; tent with foil.

2. Add garlic to drippings in skillet; cook and stir 1 minute. Stir in beans, tomatoes with juice, vinegar and 2 teaspoons minced rosemary; bring to a boil. Reduce heat to medium-low; cook 5 minutes, stirring occasionally.

3. Divide bean mixture among four plates; top with lamb. Garnish with additional rosemary.

Makes 4 servings

SKILLET LASAGNA WITH VEGETABLES

8 ounces hot Italian turkey sausage, casings removed

8 ounces ground turkey

2 stalks celery, sliced

⅓ cup chopped onion

2 cups marinara sauce

1⅓ cups water

4 ounces uncooked bowtie pasta

1 medium zucchini, halved lengthwise, then cut crosswise into ½-inch slices

¾ cup chopped green or yellow bell pepper

½ cup (2 ounces) shredded mozzarella cheese

½ cup ricotta cheese

2 tablespoons grated Parmesan cheese

1. Heat large skillet over medium-high heat. Add sausage, ground turkey, celery and onion; cook and stir 6 to 8 minutes or until turkey is no longer pink. Stir in marinara sauce and water; bring to a boil. Stir in pasta. Reduce heat to medium-low; cover and cook 12 minutes.

2. Stir in zucchini and bell pepper; cover and cook 2 minutes. Uncover; cook 4 to 6 minutes or until vegetables are crisp-tender.

3. Sprinkle with mozzarella. Combine ricotta and Parmesan in small bowl; mix well. Drop by rounded teaspoonfuls over pasta mixture in skillet. Remove from heat; cover and let stand 10 minutes.

Makes 6 servings

AUSSIE CHICKEN

½ cup honey

½ cup Dijon mustard

2 tablespoons vegetable oil, divided

1 teaspoon lemon juice

4 boneless skinless chicken breasts (about 6 ounces each)

Salt and black pepper

1 tablespoon butter

2 cups sliced mushrooms

4 slices bacon, cooked

½ cup (2 ounces) shredded Cheddar cheese

½ cup (2 ounces) shredded Monterey Jack cheese

Chopped fresh parsley

1. Whisk honey, mustard, 1 tablespoon oil and lemon juice in medium bowl until well blended. Remove half of marinade mixture to use as sauce; cover and refrigerate until ready to serve.

2. Place chicken in large resealable food storage bag. Pour remaining half of marinade over chicken; seal bag and turn to coat. Refrigerate at least 2 hours.

3. Preheat oven to 375°F. Remove chicken from marinade; discard marinade. Heat remaining 1 tablespoon oil in large ovenproof skillet over medium-high heat. Add chicken; cook 3 to 4 minutes per side or until golden brown. (Chicken will not be cooked through.) Remove chicken to plate; sprinkle with salt and pepper.

4. Heat butter in same skillet over medium-high heat. Add mushrooms; cook 8 minutes or until mushrooms begin to brown, stirring occasionally and scraping up browned bits from bottom of skillet. Season with salt and pepper. Return chicken to skillet; spoon mushrooms over chicken. Top with bacon; sprinkle with Cheddar and Monterey Jack.

5. Bake 8 to 10 minutes or until chicken is no longer pink in center and cheeses are melted. Sprinkle with parsley; serve with reserved honey-mustard mixture.

Makes 4 servings

PORK AND CORN BREAD STUFFING SKILLET

½ teaspoon paprika

¼ teaspoon salt

¼ teaspoon garlic powder

¼ teaspoon black pepper

4 bone-in pork chops (6 to 8 ounces each)

2 tablespoons butter

1½ cups chopped onions

¾ cup thinly sliced celery

¾ cup matchstick carrots*

¼ cup chopped fresh Italian parsley

1 can (about 14 ounces) chicken broth

4 cups corn bread stuffing mix

Matchstick carrots (sometimes called shredded carrots) can be found near other prepared vegetables in the supermarket produce section.

1. Preheat oven to 350°F.

2. Combine paprika, salt, garlic powder and pepper in small bowl; sprinkle over both sides of pork chops.

3. Melt butter in large ovenproof skillet over medium-high heat. Add pork; cook 2 minutes per side or just until browned. Remove to plate.

4. Add onions, celery, carrots and parsley to skillet; cook and stir 4 minutes or until onions are translucent. Stir in broth; bring to a boil. Remove from heat; add stuffing mix and fluff with fork. Arrange pork on top of stuffing mixture.

5. Cover and bake 25 minutes or until pork is barely pink in center.

Makes 4 servings

PAN-ROASTED PIKE WITH BUTTERY BREAD CRUMBS

6 tablespoons butter, divided

2 cloves garlic, minced

⅓ cup plain dry bread crumbs

½ teaspoon salt, divided

4 tablespoons chopped fresh parsley

4 pike fillets or other medium-firm white fish (about 6 ounces each)

⅛ teaspoon black pepper

2 tablespoons lemon juice

1. Preheat oven to 400°F.

2. Melt 2 tablespoons butter in small nonstick skillet over medium-high heat. Add garlic; cook and stir 1 minute or just until lightly browned. Add bread crumbs and ⅛ teaspoon salt; cook and stir 1 minute. Transfer to small bowl; stir in parsley.

3. Melt 1 tablespoon butter in large ovenproof skillet over medium-high heat. Sprinkle fish with ¼ teaspoon salt and pepper. Add to skillet, flesh side down; cook 1 minute. Remove from heat; turn fish and top with bread crumb mixture. Transfer to oven; roast 8 to 10 minutes or until fish begins to flake when tested with fork.

4. Wipe out small skillet with paper towel; heat over medium heat. Add remaining 3 tablespoons butter; cook 3 to 4 minutes or until melted and lightly browned, stirring occasionally. Stir in lemon juice and remaining ⅛ teaspoon salt. Spoon over fish just before serving.

Makes 4 servings

CHICKEN SCARPIELLO

3 tablespoons extra virgin olive oil, divided

1 pound spicy Italian sausage, cut into 1-inch pieces

1 whole chicken (about 3 pounds), cut into 10 pieces

1 teaspoon salt, divided

1 large onion, chopped

2 red, yellow or orange bell peppers, cut into ¼-inch strips

3 cloves garlic, minced

½ cup dry white wine

½ cup chicken broth

½ cup coarsely chopped seeded hot cherry peppers

½ cup liquid from cherry pepper jar

1 teaspoon dried oregano

Additional salt and black pepper

¼ cup chopped fresh Italian parsley

1. Heat 1 tablespoon oil in large skillet over medium-high heat. Add sausage; cook about 10 minutes or until well browned on all sides, stirring occasionally. Remove sausage from skillet; set aside.

2. Heat 1 tablespoon oil in same skillet. Sprinkle chicken with ½ teaspoon salt; arrange skin side down in single layer in skillet (cook in batches, if necessary). Cook about 6 minutes per side or until browned. Remove chicken from skillet; set aside. Drain oil from skillet.

3. Heat remaining 1 tablespoon oil in skillet. Add onion and ½ teaspoon salt; cook and stir 2 minutes or until onion is softened, scraping up browned bits from bottom of skillet. Add bell peppers and garlic; cook and stir 5 minutes. Stir in wine; cook until liquid is reduced by half. Stir in broth, cherry peppers, cherry pepper liquid and oregano. Season with additional salt and black pepper; bring to a simmer.

4. Return sausage and chicken along with any accumulated juices to skillet. Cover skillet; simmer 10 minutes. Uncover; simmer 15 minutes or until chicken is cooked through (165°F). Sprinkle with parsley.

Makes 6 servings

PORK CHOPS WITH BELL PEPPERS AND SWEET POTATO

4 **pork loin chops (about 1 pound), cut about ½ inch thick**

1 **teaspoon lemon-pepper seasoning**

½ **cup water**

1 **tablespoon lemon juice**

1 **teaspoon dried fines herbes, crushed**

½ **teaspoon beef bouillon granules**

1¼ **cups red or yellow bell pepper strips or a combination**

1 **cup sliced sweet potato, cut into 1-inch pieces**

¾ **cup sliced onion**

4 **cups hot cooked rice**

1. Trim fat from chops; discard. Rub both sides of chops with lemon-pepper seasoning. Coat large skillet with nonstick cooking spray. Heat skillet over medium-high heat. Add chops; cook 5 minutes or until browned on both sides.

2. Combine water, lemon juice, fines herbes and bouillon in small bowl; stir to blend. Pour over chops. Reduce heat to medium-low. Cover; simmer 5 minutes.

3. Add bell peppers, sweet potato and onion to skillet; return to a boil. Reduce heat. Cover; simmer 10 to 15 minutes or until chops are slightly pink in center and vegetables are crisp-tender. Remove chops and vegetables from skillet; keep warm.

4. Bring remaining juices in skillet to a boil over high heat. Reduce heat to medium. Cook and stir 6 to 8 minutes or until mixture slightly thickens, stirring occasionally. Arrange chops and vegetables on large serving plate; spoon sauce over chops and vegetables. Serve with rice.

Makes 4 servings

Sheet Pan

ROAST CHICKEN AND POTATOES CATALAN

2 tablespoons olive oil

2 tablespoons lemon juice

1 teaspoon dried thyme

½ teaspoon salt

¼ teaspoon ground red pepper

¼ teaspoon ground saffron *or* ½ teaspoon crushed saffron threads or turmeric

2 large baking potatoes (about 1½ pounds), cut into 1½-inch pieces

4 skinless bone-in chicken breasts (about 8 ounces each)

1 cup sliced red bell pepper

1 cup frozen peas, thawed

Lemon wedges

1. Preheat oven to 400°F. Spray baking sheet with nonstick cooking spray.

2. Combine oil, lemon juice, thyme, salt, ground red pepper and saffron in large bowl; mix well. Add potatoes; toss to coat.

3. Arrange potatoes in single layer around edges of baking sheet. Place chicken in center of baking sheet; brush both sides of chicken with remaining oil mixture in bowl.

4. Roast 20 minutes. Turn potatoes; baste chicken with pan juices. Add bell pepper; continue roasting 20 minutes or until chicken is no longer pink in center, juices run clear and potatoes are browned. Stir peas into potato mixture; roast 5 minutes or until heated through. Garnish with lemon wedges.

Makes 4 servings

RESTAURANT-STYLE BABY BACK RIBS

1¼ cups water

1 cup white vinegar

⅔ cup packed dark brown sugar

½ cup tomato paste

1 tablespoon yellow mustard

1½ teaspoons salt

1 teaspoon liquid smoke

1 teaspoon onion powder

½ teaspoon garlic powder

½ teaspoon paprika

2 racks pork baby back ribs (3½ to 4 pounds total)

1. Combine water, vinegar, brown sugar, tomato paste, mustard, salt, liquid smoke, onion powder, garlic powder and paprika in medium saucepan; bring to a boil over medium heat. Reduce heat to medium-low; cook 30 minutes or until sauce thickens, stirring occasionally.

2. Preheat oven to 300°F. Place each rack of ribs on large sheet of heavy-duty foil. Brush some of sauce over ribs, covering completely. Fold down edges of foil tightly to seal and create packet; arrange packets on baking sheet, seam sides up.

3. Bake 2 hours. Preheat broiler. Carefully drain off excess liquid from rib packets.

4. Brush ribs with sauce; broil about 5 minutes per side or until beginning to char, brushing with sauce once or twice during cooking. Serve with remaining sauce.

Makes 4 servings

PARMESAN-CRUSTED TILAPIA

⅔ cup plus
   3 tablespoons
   grated Parmesan
   cheese, divided

⅔ cup panko bread
   crumbs

⅓ cup prepared
   Alfredo sauce
   (refrigerated or
   jarred)

1½ teaspoons dried
   parsley flakes

4 tilapia fillets
   (6 ounces each)

Shaved Parmesan
   cheese (optional)

Minced fresh
   parsley (optional)

1. Preheat oven to 425°F. Line baking sheet with foil; spray foil with nonstick cooking spray.

2. Combine ⅔ cup grated cheese and panko in medium bowl; mix well. Combine Alfredo sauce, remaining 3 tablespoons grated cheese and parsley flakes in small bowl; mix well. Spread sauce mixture over top of fish, coating in thick even layer. Top with panko mixture, pressing in gently to adhere. Place fish on prepared baking sheet.

3. Bake on top rack of oven about 15 minutes or until crust is golden brown and fish begins to flake when tested with fork. Garnish with shaved Parmesan and fresh parsley.

Makes 4 servings

MOUNDED MINI MEAT LOAVES

1   can (8 ounces)
    tomato sauce,
    divided

¼   cup ketchup

2   teaspoons
    Worcestershire
    sauce, divided

1   pound ground
    beef

1   cup cooked and
    cooled quinoa,
    any variety*

1   cup chopped bell
    green pepper

½   cup finely
    chopped onion

2   eggs, beaten

¾   teaspoon salt

½   teaspoon black
    pepper

*Cook ⅓ cup uncooked
quinoa with ⅔ cup
water according to
package directions.
Place cooked quinoa
in fine-mesh sieve; run
under cold running
water to cool quickly.
Drain well.*

1. Preheat oven to 350°F. Generously spray baking sheet with nonstick cooking spray or line with parchment paper.

2. Combine ¼ cup tomato sauce, ketchup and ½ teaspoon Worcestershire sauce in small bowl; mix well. Set aside for topping.

3. Combine remaining tomato sauce, 1½ teaspoons Worcestershire sauce, beef, quinoa, bell pepper, onion, eggs, salt and black pepper in medium bowl; mix well. Divide mixture into four portions; shape each into individual meat loaf (about 3 inches wide, 5 inches long and 1 inch high) on prepared baking sheet. Mixture will be slightly moist.

4. Bake 35 minutes or until meat loaves are 165°F. Spoon reserved ketchup mixture over tops and sides of meat loaves; bake 10 minutes.

Makes 4 servings

HONEY LEMON GARLIC CHICKEN

2 lemons, divided

2 tablespoons butter, melted

2 tablespoons honey

3 cloves garlic, chopped

2 sprigs fresh rosemary, leaves removed from stems

1 teaspoon coarse salt

½ teaspoon black pepper

3 pounds chicken (4 bone-in skin-on chicken thighs and 4 drumsticks)

1¼ pounds unpeeled small potatoes, cut into halves or quarters

1. Preheat oven to 375°F. Grate peel and squeeze juice from 1 lemon. Cut remaining lemon into slices.

2. Combine lemon peel, lemon juice, butter, honey, garlic, rosemary leaves, salt and pepper in small bowl; mix well.

3. Combine chicken, potatoes and lemon slices on baking sheet. Pour butter mixture over chicken and potatoes; toss to coat. Spread in single layer.

4. Bake about 1 hour or until potatoes are tender and chicken is cooked through (165°F). Cover loosely with foil if chicken skin is becoming too dark.

Makes 4 servings

MEXICAN PIZZA

1 **package (about 14 ounces) refrigerated pizza dough**

1 **cup chunky salsa**

1 **teaspoon ground cumin**

1 **cup canned black beans, rinsed and drained**

1 **cup frozen corn, thawed**

½ **cup sliced green onions**

1½ **cups (6 ounces) shredded Mexican cheese blend**

½ **cup chopped fresh cilantro (optional)**

1. Preheat oven to 425°F. Spray baking sheet with nonstick cooking spray. Unroll dough on baking sheet; press dough to edges of pan.

2. Bake 8 minutes. Combine salsa and cumin in small bowl; spread over partially baked crust. Top with beans, corn and green onions. Bake 8 minutes or until crust is deep golden brown.

3. Sprinkle with cheese; bake 2 minutes or until cheese is melted. Garnish with cilantro.

Makes 8 servings

HERB-ROASTED DIJON LAMB AND VEGETABLES

20 cloves garlic, peeled (about 2 medium heads)

¼ cup Dijon mustard

2 tablespoons water

2 tablespoons fresh rosemary leaves

1 tablespoon fresh thyme

1¼ teaspoons salt, divided

1 teaspoon black pepper

4½ pounds boneless leg of lamb, trimmed

1 pound parsnips, cut diagonally into ½-inch pieces

1 pound carrots, cut diagonally into ½-inch pieces

2 large onions, cut into ½-inch wedges

3 tablespoons extra virgin olive oil, divided

1. Combine garlic, mustard, water, rosemary, thyme, ¾ teaspoon salt and pepper in food processor; process until smooth. Spoon mixture over top and sides of lamb. Cover and refrigerate at least 8 hours.

2. Preheat oven to 500°F. Line baking sheet with foil; top with broiler rack. Spray rack with nonstick cooking spray. Combine parsnips, carrots, onions and 2 tablespoons oil in large bowl; toss to coat. Spread on broiler rack; top with lamb.

3. Roast 15 minutes. *Reduce oven temperature to 325°F.* Roast 1 hour 20 minutes or until lamb is 155°F for medium or to desired doneness.

4. Remove lamb to cutting board; tent with foil. Let stand 10 minutes before slicing. Continue roasting vegetables 10 minutes.

5. Transfer vegetables to large bowl. Add remaining 1 tablespoon oil and ½ teaspoon salt; toss to coat. Thinly slice lamb; serve with vegetables.

Makes 6 servings

ROASTED SALMON WITH NEW POTATOES AND RED ONIONS

¼ cup chicken broth

1 tablespoon olive oil

1½ pounds small new potatoes, cut into halves

1 medium red onion, cut into ¼-inch wedges

6 salmon fillets (about 4 ounces each)

¾ teaspoon salt

½ teaspoon black pepper

Sprigs fresh tarragon or dill (optional)

1. Preheat oven to 400°F. Spray baking sheet with nonstick cooking spray.

2. Combine broth and oil in small bowl. Combine potatoes and half of broth mixture on prepared baking sheet; toss to coat.

3. Roast 20 minutes. Add onion and remaining broth mixture to baking sheet; toss to coat. Push vegetables to edges of baking sheet; place fish in center. Sprinkle fish and vegetables with salt and pepper. Roast 10 to 15 minutes or until center of fish is opaque and vegetables are tender. Garnish with tarragon.

Makes 6 servings

ROSEMARY PORK TENDERLOIN AND VEGETABLES

¼ cup chicken broth

1 tablespoon olive or vegetable oil

3 large parsnips, peeled and cut diagonally into ½-inch slices

2 cups baby carrots

1 red bell pepper, cut into ¾-inch pieces

1 medium onion, cut into wedges

2 small pork tenderloins (12 ounces each)

2 tablespoons Dijon or spicy Dijon mustard

2 teaspoons dried rosemary

¾ teaspoon salt

½ teaspoon black pepper

1. Preheat oven to 400°F. Spray baking sheet with nonstick cooking spray.

2. Combine broth and oil in small bowl. Combine parsnips, carrots and 3 tablespoons broth mixture on prepared baking sheet; toss to coat. Spread vegetables in single layer.

3. Roast vegetables 10 minutes. Add bell pepper, onion and remaining broth mixture to baking sheet; toss to coat. Push vegetables to edges of baking sheet. Place pork in center of baking sheet; spread with mustard. Sprinkle pork and vegetables with rosemary, salt and black pepper.

4. Roast 25 to 30 minutes or until vegetables are tender and pork is 145°F. Remove pork to cutting board; tent with foil. Let stand 5 minutes before slicing. Cut into ½-inch slices; serve with vegetables and any juices from pan.

Makes 6 servings

CHORIZO ARTICHOKE KABOBS WITH MUSTARD VINAIGRETTE

1 can (about 14 ounces) large artichoke hearts, drained
2 fully cooked chorizo-flavored chicken sausages or andouille sausages (3 ounces each)
3 tablespoons olive oil
2 teaspoons white wine vinegar
1 teaspoon Dijon mustard
   Salt and black pepper

1. Preheat broiler. Soak six wooden skewers in water 20 minutes. Line baking sheet with heavy-duty foil.

2. Cut artichoke hearts in half. Cut each sausage diagonally into 6 slices. Arrange 2 artichoke pieces and 2 sausage slices on each skewer. Place skewers on prepared baking sheet.

3. Broil 4 inches from heat 4 minutes or until artichokes are hot and sausage is browned.

4. Meanwhile, whisk oil, vinegar and mustard in small bowl until blended. Season with salt and pepper. Serve with kabobs.

Makes 2 servings

Slow Cooker

HEARTY VEGETARIAN MAC AND CHEESE

1 can (about 14 ounces) stewed tomatoes, undrained

1½ cups prepared Alfredo sauce

1½ cups (6 ounces) shredded mozzarella cheese, divided

8 ounces uncooked whole grain pasta (medium shells or penne), cooked until al dente

7 ounces Italian-flavored vegetarian sausage links, cut into ¼-inch slices

¾ cup fresh basil leaves, thinly sliced, divided

½ cup vegetable broth

½ teaspoon salt

2 tablespoons grated Parmesan cheese

1. Spray slow cooker with nonstick cooking spray. Combine tomatoes, Alfredo sauce, 1 cup mozzarella, pasta, sausage, ½ cup basil, broth and salt in slow cooker; mix well. Top with remaining ½ cup mozzarella and Parmesan.

2. Cover; cook on LOW 3½ hours or on HIGH 2 hours. Top with remaining ¼ cup basil.

Makes 6 servings

BRAISED SHORT RIBS WITH SWEET POTATOES

1 tablespoon olive oil

3 pounds bone-in beef short ribs, trimmed

1 teaspoon ground cumin, divided

1 teaspoon salt

½ teaspoon black pepper

2 medium onions, halved and thinly sliced

10 cloves garlic, thinly sliced

2 tablespoons balsamic vinegar

2 tablespoons honey

1 whole cinnamon stick

2 whole star anise pods

2 large sweet potatoes, peeled and cut into ¾-inch pieces

1 cup beef broth

1. Heat oil in large skillet over medium-high heat. Season ribs with ½ teaspoon cumin, salt and pepper. Add to skillet; cook 8 minutes or until browned, turning occasionally. Remove to plate.

2. Add onions and garlic to skillet; cook over medium heat 12 to 14 minutes or until onions are lightly browned. Stir in vinegar; cook 1 minute. Add remaining ½ teaspoon cumin, honey, cinnamon stick and star anise; cook and stir 30 seconds. Transfer mixture to slow cooker. Stir in sweet potatoes; top with ribs. Pour in broth.

3. Cover; cook on LOW 8 to 9 hours or until meat is falling off the bones. Remove and discard bones, cinnamon stick and star anise. Turn off heat; let stand 5 to 10 minutes. Skim off fat before serving.

Makes 4 servings

PORK AND TOMATO RAGOÛT

2 pounds cubed pork stew meat

¼ cup all-purpose flour

3 tablespoons vegetable oil

1¼ cups dry white wine

2 pounds unpeeled red potatoes, cut into ½-inch pieces

1 can (about 14 ounces) diced tomatoes

1 cup finely chopped onion

1 cup water

½ cup finely chopped celery

2 cloves garlic, minced

½ teaspoon black pepper

1 cinnamon stick

3 tablespoons chopped fresh parsley

1. Combine pork and flour in large bowl; toss to coat. Heat oil in large skillet over medium-high heat. Add pork; cook until browned. Transfer to slow cooker.

2. Add wine to skillet; bring to a boil, scraping up browned bits from bottom of skillet. Pour into slow cooker. Add potatoes, tomatoes, onion, water, celery, garlic, pepper and cinnamon stick.

3. Cover; cook on LOW 6 to 8 hours or until pork and potatoes are tender. Remove and discard cinnamon stick. Adjust seasonings, if desired. Sprinkle with parsley.

Makes 6 servings

TIP Vegetables such as potatoes and carrots can sometimes take longer to cook in a slow cooker than meat. Place cut vegetables along the side of the slow cooker when possible.

RUSTIC ITALIAN WHITE BEAN SOUP

10 cups chicken broth

1 package (16 ounces) dried Great Northern beans, rinsed and sorted

1 can (about 14 ounces) diced tomatoes

1 large onion, chopped

3 carrots, chopped

6 ounces bacon, crisp-cooked and chopped

4 cloves garlic, minced

1 sprig fresh rosemary *or* 1 teaspoon dried rosemary

1 teaspoon black pepper

1. Combine broth, beans, tomatoes, onion, carrots, bacon, garlic, rosemary and pepper in slow cooker.

2. Cover; cook on LOW 8 hours. Remove and discard rosemary before serving.

Makes 8 to 10 servings

SERVING SUGGESTION Place slices of toasted Italian bread in soup bowls; drizzle with olive oil. Ladle soup over bread.

GREEK-STYLE MEATBALLS AND SPINACH

½ cup old-fashioned oats

¼ cup minced onion

1 clove garlic, minced

¼ teaspoon dried oregano

⅛ teaspoon black pepper

1 egg, lightly beaten

8 ounces ground lamb

1 cup beef broth

½ teaspoon salt

½ cup plain yogurt

1 teaspoon all-purpose flour

4 cups baby spinach, coarsely chopped

3 cups hot cooked egg noodles

1. Combine oats, onion, garlic, oregano and pepper in medium bowl; mix well. Stir in egg. Add lamb; mix gently. Shape mixture into 16 balls; place in slow cooker. Add broth and salt.

2. Cover; cook on LOW 6 hours. Whisk yogurt and flour in small bowl until blended. Whisk about ¼ cup hot liquid from slow cooker into yogurt mixture. Stir yogurt mixture into liquid in slow cooker. Add spinach.

3. Cover; cook on LOW 10 minutes or until heated through. Serve over noodles.

Makes 4 servings

NEW ENGLAND POT ROAST

1 beef chuck pot roast (about 2½ pounds), trimmed and cut into bite-size pieces

Salt and black pepper

3 unpeeled medium baking potatoes (about 1 pound), cut into quarters

2 large carrots, cut into ¾-inch slices

2 stalks celery, cut into ¾-inch slices

1 medium onion, sliced

1 large parsnip, cut into ¾-inch slices

2 bay leaves

1 teaspoon dried rosemary

½ teaspoon dried thyme

½ cup beef broth

1. Season beef with salt and pepper. Combine potatoes, carrots, celery, onion, parsnip, bay leaves, rosemary and thyme in slow cooker. Place beef over vegetables. Pour broth over beef.

2. Cover; cook on LOW 8½ to 9 hours or until beef is fork-tender. Remove beef and vegetables to serving platter. Remove and discard bay leaves.

Makes 6 to 8 servings

TIP To make gravy, pour cooking liquid into 2-cup measure; let stand 5 minutes. Skim off fat. Bring cooking liquid to a boil in small saucepan over medium-high heat. For each cup, stir ¼ cup cold water into 2 tablespoons all-purpose flour in small bowl until smooth. Add flour mixture to boiling cooking liquid; cook and stir 1 minute or until thickened.

SWEET AND SOUR CHICKEN

¼ cup chicken broth

2 tablespoons soy sauce

2 tablespoons hoisin sauce

1 tablespoon cider vinegar

1 tablespoon tomato paste

2 teaspoons packed brown sugar

1 clove garlic, minced

¼ teaspoon black pepper

1 pound boneless skinless chicken thighs, cut into 1-inch pieces

2 teaspoons cornstarch

2 tablespoons snipped fresh chives

Hot cooked rice

1. Combine broth, soy sauce, hoisin sauce, vinegar, tomato paste, brown sugar, garlic and pepper in slow cooker; mix well. Add chicken; stir to coat.

2. Cover; cook on LOW 2½ to 3½ hours. Remove chicken to bowl with slotted spoon; keep warm.

3. Whisk cornstarch into 2 tablespoons cooking liquid in small bowl until smooth. Add to slow cooker with chives. *Turn slow cooker to HIGH.* Cook, uncovered, 2 minutes or until sauce is slightly thickened, stirring constantly. Serve chicken and sauce over rice.

Makes 4 servings

NEW MEXICAN GREEN CHILE PORK STEW

1½ pounds boneless pork shoulder, cut into 1-inch pieces

2 medium baking potatoes or sweet potatoes, peeled and cut into 1-inch pieces

1 cup chopped onion

1 cup frozen corn

1 can (4 ounces) diced mild green chiles

1 jar (16 ounces) salsa verde (green salsa)

2 teaspoons sugar

2 teaspoons ground cumin or chili powder

1 teaspoon dried oregano

Hot cooked rice

¼ cup chopped fresh cilantro (optional)

1. Combine pork, potatoes, onion, corn and chiles in slow cooker. Combine salsa, sugar, cumin and oregano in small bowl; mix well. Pour over pork and vegetables; stir gently to coat.

2. Cover; cook on LOW 6 to 8 hours or on HIGH 4 to 5 hours or until pork is tender. Serve with rice; garnish with cilantro.

Makes 6 servings

CHICKEN IN ENCHILADA SAUCE

1	can (about 14 ounces) diced tomatoes with green chiles
1	can (10 ounces) enchilada sauce
1	cup frozen or canned corn
¼	teaspoon ground cumin
¼	teaspoon red pepper flakes
⅛	teaspoon black pepper
1½	pounds boneless skinless chicken thighs, cut into bite-size pieces
2	tablespoons minced fresh cilantro
½	cup (2 ounces) shredded pepper jack cheese
	Sliced green onions (optional)

1. Combine tomatoes, enchilada sauce, corn, cumin, red pepper flakes and black pepper in slow cooker. Add chicken; mix well.

2. Cover; cook on LOW 6 to 7 hours. Stir in cilantro. Sprinkle with cheese; garnish with green onions.

Makes 4 servings

BARLEY AND SAUSAGE GUMBO

1 small onion, chopped

1 large green bell pepper, chopped

1 cup frozen sliced okra

1 medium stalk celery, chopped

1 clove garlic, minced

1 cup chicken broth

1 cup tomato purée

¼ cup uncooked pearl barley

1 teaspoon dried oregano

¾ teaspoon salt

⅛ teaspoon red pepper flakes

2 andouille sausages (3 ounces each), cut into ½-inch slices

1. Combine onion, bell pepper, okra, celery and garlic in slow cooker. Add broth, tomato purée, barley, oregano, salt and red pepper flakes; mix well. Stir in sausages.

2. Cover; cook on LOW 5 to 6 hours. Let stand 5 minutes before serving.

Makes 4 servings

Pressure Cooker

MU SHU TURKEY

1 jar (about 7 ounces) plum sauce, divided

¼ cup orange juice (juice of 1 medium orange)

¼ cup finely chopped onion

1 tablespoon minced fresh ginger

¼ teaspoon salt

¼ teaspoon ground cinnamon

1 pound boneless turkey breast, cut into thin strips

6 (7-inch) flour tortillas

3 cups coleslaw mix

1. Combine ⅓ cup plum sauce, orange juice, onion, ginger, salt and cinnamon in pot; mix well. Add turkey, stir to coat.

2. Secure lid and move pressure release valve to sealing or locked position. Cook at high pressure 4 minutes.

3. When cooking is complete, press Cancel and use quick release.

4. Press Sauté; cook 2 to 3 minutes or until sauce is reduced and thickens slightly.

5. Spread remaining jarred plum sauce over tortillas; top with turkey and coleslaw mix. Fold bottom edge of tortillas over filling; fold in sides and roll up to completely enclose filling. Serve with remaining cooking sauce for dipping.

Makes 6 servings

CHICKEN TORTILLA SOUP

2 cans (about 14 ounces each) diced tomatoes

1½ pounds boneless skinless chicken thighs

1 onion, chopped

½ cup chicken broth

1 can (4 ounces) diced green chiles

2 cloves garlic, minced

1 teaspoon salt

1 teaspoon ground cumin

¼ teaspoon black pepper

4 corn tortillas, cut into ¼-inch strips

2 tablespoons chopped fresh cilantro

½ cup (2 ounces) shredded Monterey Jack cheese

1 avocado, diced and tossed with lime juice

Lime wedges

1. Combine tomatoes, chicken, onion, broth, chiles, garlic, salt, cumin and pepper in pot; mix well.

2. Secure lid and move pressure release valve to sealing or locked position. Cook at high pressure 9 minutes.

3. When cooking is complete, use natural release for 10 minutes, then release remaining pressure.

4. Remove chicken to plate; shred into bite-size pieces when cool enough to handle. Stir into soup.

5. Press Sauté; add tortillas and cilantro to soup. Cook and stir 2 minutes or until heated through. Top with cheese, avocado and squeeze of lime juice. Serve immediately.

Makes 4 to 6 servings

CLASSIC BEEF STEW

2½ pounds cubed beef stew meat

¼ cup all-purpose flour

1½ teaspoons salt, divided

2 tablespoons olive oil, divided

1 cup beef broth

1 medium onion, chopped

1 ounce dried oyster mushrooms, chopped

2 teaspoons garlic powder

1 teaspoon *each* dried basil and dried oregano

½ teaspoon dried rosemary

½ teaspoon dried marjoram

½ teaspoon dried sage

½ teaspoon dried thyme

8 fingerling potatoes, halved lengthwise

1 cup baby carrots

Black pepper

Chopped fresh Italian parsley (optional)

1. Combine beef, flour and ½ teaspoon salt in large resealable food storage bag; toss to coat. Press Sauté; heat 1 tablespoon oil in pot. Add half of beef; cook about 5 minutes or until browned. Remove to plate; repeat with remaining oil and beef.

2. Add broth, onion, mushrooms, garlic powder, remaining 1 teaspoon salt, basil, oregano, rosemary, marjoram, sage and thyme to pot; mix well. Return beef to pot. Secure lid and move pressure release valve to sealing or locked position. Cook at high pressure 30 minutes.

3. When cooking is complete, press Cancel and use quick release.

4. Add potatoes and carrots to pot. Secure lid and move pressure release valve to sealing or locked position. Cook at high pressure 10 minutes.

5. When cooking is complete, press Cancel and use quick release. Season with additional salt and pepper, if desired. Garnish with parsley.

Makes 8 servings

SWEET POTATO AND BLACK BEAN CHILI

1	tablespoon olive oil
1	large onion, chopped
4	teaspoons chili powder
2	cloves garlic, minced
1	teaspoon salt
1	teaspoon chipotle chili powder
½	teaspoon ground cumin
2	cans (about 15 ounces each) black beans, rinsed and drained
1	large sweet potato, peeled and cut into ½-inch pieces
1	can (about 14 ounces) diced tomatoes
1	can (about 14 ounces) crushed tomatoes
1½	cups vegetable broth
	Optional toppings: sliced green onions, shredded Cheddar cheese and/or tortilla chips

1. Press Sauté; heat oil in pot. Add onion; cook and stir 3 minutes or until softened. Add chili powder, garlic, salt, chipotle chili powder and cumin; cook and stir 1 minute. Stir in beans, sweet potato, diced tomatoes, crushed tomatoes and broth; mix well.

2. Secure lid and move pressure release valve to sealing or locked position. Cook at high pressure 4 minutes.

3. When cooking is complete, press Cancel and use quick release.

4. Press Sauté; cook 3 to 5 minutes or until chili thickens to desired consistency, stirring frequently. Serve with desired toppings.

Makes 6 servings

HOT AND SWEET SAUSAGE SANDWICHES

1½ cups pasta sauce

1 large sweet onion, cut into ¼-inch slices

1 medium green bell pepper, cut into ½-inch slices

1 medium red bell pepper, cut into ½-inch slices

1½ tablespoons packed dark brown sugar

1 package (16 ounces) hot Italian sausage links (5 sausages)

5 Italian rolls, split

1. Combine pasta sauce, onion, bell peppers and brown sugar in pot; mix well. Add sausages to pot; spoon some of sauce mixture over sausages.

2. Secure lid and move pressure release valve to sealing or locked position. Cook at high pressure 5 minutes.

3. When cooking is complete, use natural release for 10 minutes, then release remaining pressure. Remove sausages to plate; tent with foil.

4. Press Sauté; cook 10 minutes or until sauce is reduced by one third, stirring occasionally. Serve sausages in rolls; top with sauce.

Makes 5 servings

TIP If you have any leftover sauce, refrigerate or freeze it and serve over pasta or polenta. Top with grated Parmesan cheese.

MUSHROOM BARLEY SOUP

2 tablespoons olive oil

1 onion, chopped

2 carrots, chopped

2 stalks celery, chopped

3 cloves garlic, minced

1 teaspoon salt

½ teaspoon dried thyme

½ teaspoon black pepper

5 cups vegetable or chicken broth

1 package (16 ounces) sliced mushrooms

½ cup uncooked pearl barley

½ ounce dried porcini or shiitake mushrooms

1. Press Sauté; heat oil in pot. Add onion, carrots and celery; cook and stir 5 minutes or until vegetables are softened. Add garlic, salt, thyme and pepper; cook and stir 1 minute. Stir in broth, sliced mushrooms, barley and dried mushrooms; mix well.

2. Secure lid and move pressure release valve to sealing or locked position. Cook at high pressure 22 minutes.

3. When cooking is complete, use natural release for 10 minutes, then release remaining pressure.

Makes 6 to 8 servings

TURKEY ROPA VIEJA

1 tablespoon olive oil

1 onion, thinly sliced

1 green bell pepper, chopped

1 clove garlic, minced

¾ teaspoon ground cumin

½ teaspoon dried oregano

2 medium tomatoes, chopped

1 can (8 ounces) tomato sauce

⅓ cup sliced pimiento-stuffed green olives

½ teaspoon salt

¼ teaspoon black pepper

1 pound turkey tenderloins (2 large or 3 small) *or* 1½ pounds boneless turkey breast, cut into 3 to 4 pieces

1 tablespoon lemon juice

Hot cooked rice and beans (optional)

1. Press Sauté; heat oil in pot. Add onion and bell pepper; cook and stir 3 minutes or until softened. Add garlic, cumin and oregano; cook and stir 30 seconds. Stir in tomatoes, tomato sauce, olives, salt and black pepper; mix well. Add turkey to pot, pressing into tomato mixture.

2. Secure lid and move pressure release valve to sealing or locked position. Cook at high pressure 20 minutes.

3. When cooking is complete, use natural release for 10 minutes, then release remaining pressure. Remove turkey to plate.

4. Press Sauté; cook 10 to 15 minutes or until sauce is reduced by one third.

5. Meanwhile, shred turkey into bite-size pieces when cool enough to handle. Add shredded turkey and lemon juice to sauce; mix well. Serve with rice and beans, if desired.

Makes 4 servings

BEEF POT ROAST DINNER

2 cloves garlic, minced

1 teaspoon salt

1 teaspoon herbes de Provence*

1 teaspoon ground sage

1 teaspoon ground cumin

1 teaspoon black pepper

1 beef eye of round roast (about 2½ pounds), trimmed

2 tablespoons olive oil

1 cup beef broth

4 small turnips, peeled and cut into wedges

12 medium fresh brussels sprouts, trimmed

2 cups halved small new red potatoes

2 cups baby carrots

1 cup pearl onions, skins removed *or* 1 large onion, cut into wedges

*You may substitute ¼ teaspoon **each** dried rosemary, thyme, sage and savory.*

1. Combine garlic, salt, herbes de Provence, sage, cumin and pepper in small bowl; mix well. Rub mixture into all sides of beef.

2. Press Sauté; heat oil in pot. Add beef; cook about 5 minutes or until browned on all sides. Remove to plate. Stir in broth, scraping up browned bits from bottom of pot. Place rack in pot; place beef on rack.

3. Secure lid and move pressure release valve to sealing or locked position. Cook at high pressure 50 minutes.

4. When cooking is complete, use natural release for 5 minutes, then release remaining pressure.

5. Add turnips, brussels sprouts, potatoes, carrots and onions to pot. Secure lid and move pressure release valve to sealing or locked position. Cook at high pressure 10 minutes.

6. When cooking is complete, press Cancel and use quick release. Serve beef and vegetables with cooking liquid or thicken sauce, if desired.

Makes 4 to 6 servings

SPICY SQUASH AND CHICKEN SOUP

1 tablespoon vegetable oil

1 small onion, finely chopped

1 stalk celery, finely chopped

2 cups chicken broth

2 cups cubed butternut squash (1-inch pieces)

1 can (about 14 ounces) diced tomatoes with chiles

8 ounces boneless skinless chicken thighs, cut into ½-inch pieces

½ teaspoon salt

½ teaspoon ground ginger

⅛ teaspoon ground cumin

⅛ teaspoon black pepper

2 teaspoons lime juice

½ to 1 teaspoon hot pepper sauce

Fresh cilantro or parsley sprigs (optional)

1. Press Sauté; heat oil in pot. Add onion and celery; cook and stir 4 minutes or until vegetables are softened. Add broth, squash, tomatoes, chicken, salt, ginger, cumin and black pepper; mix well.

2. Secure lid and move pressure release valve to sealing or locked position. Cook at high pressure 5 minutes.

3. When cooking is complete, use natural release for 10 minutes, then release remaining pressure.

4. Stir in lime juice and hot pepper sauce; garnish with cilantro.

Makes 4 servings

Index

METRIC CONVERSION CHART

VOLUME MEASUREMENTS (dry)

1/8 teaspoon = 0.5 mL
1/4 teaspoon = 1 mL
1/2 teaspoon = 2 mL
3/4 teaspoon = 4 mL
1 teaspoon = 5 mL
1 tablespoon = 15 mL
2 tablespoons = 30 mL
1/4 cup = 60 mL
1/3 cup = 75 mL
1/2 cup = 125 mL
2/3 cup = 150 mL
3/4 cup = 175 mL
1 cup = 250 mL
2 cups = 1 pint = 500 mL
3 cups = 750 mL
4 cups = 1 quart = 1 L

VOLUME MEASUREMENTS (fluid)

1 fluid ounce (2 tablespoons) = 30 mL
4 fluid ounces (1/2 cup) = 125 mL
8 fluid ounces (1 cup) = 250 mL
12 fluid ounces (1 1/2 cups) = 375 mL
16 fluid ounces (2 cups) = 500 mL

WEIGHTS (mass)

1/2 ounce = 15 g
1 ounce = 30 g
3 ounces = 90 g
4 ounces = 120 g
8 ounces = 225 g
10 ounces = 285 g
12 ounces = 360 g
16 ounces = 1 pound = 450 g

DIMENSIONS

1/16 inch = 2 mm
1/8 inch = 3 mm
1/4 inch = 6 mm
1/2 inch = 1.5 cm
3/4 inch = 2 cm
1 inch = 2.5 cm

OVEN TEMPERATURES

250°F = 120°C
275°F = 140°C
300°F = 150°C
325°F = 160°C
350°F = 180°C
375°F = 190°C
400°F = 200°C
425°F = 220°C
450°F = 230°C

BAKING PAN SIZES

Utensil	Size in Inches/Quarts	Metric Volume	Size in Centimeters
Baking or	8×8×2	2 L	20×20×5
Cake Pan	9×9×2	2.5 L	23×23×5
(square or	12×8×2	3 L	30×20×5
rectangular)	13×9×2	3.5 L	33×23×5
Loaf Pan	8×4×3	1.5 L	20×10×7
	9×5×3	2 L	23×13×7
Round Layer	8×1½	1.2 L	20×4
Cake Pan	9×1½	1.5 L	23×4
Pie Plate	8×1¼	750 mL	20×3
	9×1¼	1 L	23×3
Baking Dish	1 quart	1 L	—
or Casserole	1½ quart	1.5 L	—
	2 quart	2 L	—